Spotlight Poets

Thoughts from Within

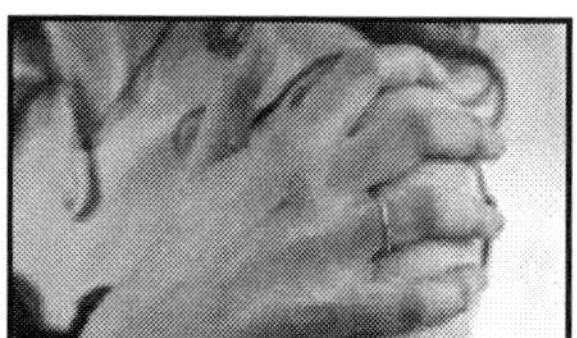
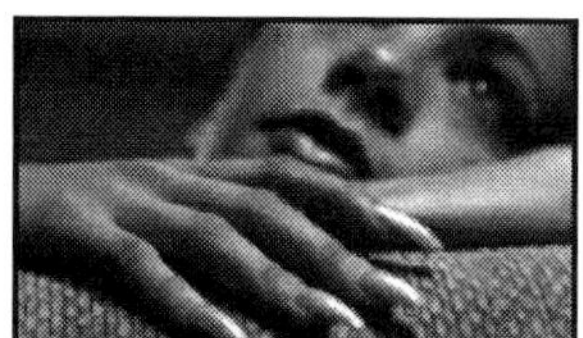

Edited by Sarah Marshall

First published in Great Britain in 2005 by
SPOTLIGHT POETS
Remus House
Coltsfoot Drive
Peterborough
PE2 9JX
Telephone: 01733 898102
Fax: 01733 313524
Website: www.forwardpress.co.uk

SB ISBN 1 84077 130 5

Foreword

As a nation of poetry writers and lovers, many of us are still surprisingly reluctant to go out and actually buy the books we cherish so much. Often when searching out the work of newer and less known authors it becomes a near impossible mission to track down the sort of books you require. In an effort to break away from the endless clutter of seemingly unrelated poems from authors we know nothing or little about; Spotlight Poets has opened up a doorway to something quite special.

Thoughts from Within is a collection of poems to be cherished forever; featuring the work of nine captivating poets each with a selection of their very best work. Placing that alongside their own personal profile gives a complete feel for the way each author works, allowing for a clearer idea of the true feelings and reasoning behind the poems.

The poems and poets have been chosen and presented in a complementary anthology that offers a variety of ideals and ideas, capable of moving the heart, mind and soul of the reader.

Sarah Marshall

Contents

The Authors & Poems

Dorothy M Mitchell

I was born in a small Yorkshire village just before the second world war, hard times, air raid shelters, sky red with fire as enemy planes bombed nearby Bradford. My dad worked as a signalman, and part-time 'Dad's Army'. Mum cleaned at the local pub. Ration books and swapping coupons was a regular occurrence, 'make do and mend' was part of life then. Dad kept chickens, grew veg in the garden, we managed.

In 1953 we moved to Evesham, I was 16 years. Married at 18. First son arrived when I was 21. My second son at 27. I was diagnosed with multiple sclerosis in my late 30s. Suffered many relapses, I was widowed at 53. My life was at a low ebb, I met a friend who asked me to go to church with her. 'The Elim Pentecostal' in Evesham. Well, I couldn't feel any worse than I did, so off I went. That was to be the turning point in my life. This was what I needed, Pastor talked to me, I cried out my pain and asked Jesus into my life.

My present hubby attended the church. He was widowed a year before me. All at church were concerned for him, he was hurting so, I know Jesus sent me there so we could be together. Pastor married us 10 years ago, I was baptised on our first wedding anniversary.

3 years ago out of the blue, poems started coming to me, gentle poems with a message, I feel the Lord is using me, I am humbled, blessed.

Each Little Soul

'Everything comes to he who waits',
This is the story I'm told,
Tell that to the boy with the big, sad, brown eyes,
Just a few grains of rice in his bowl.

Tell that to the baby who cries all alone,
In a war-ravaged country, so cold,
Tell that to a mum with a babe at her breast,
Whose life milk no longer flows.

Tell that to a young girl in nightmare's hell,
As into slavery she's sold,
To abuse unthinkable, her innocence gone,
Relieved only when death takes its toll.

Tell the millions of babies starving each day,
They never will live to grow old,
I pray that the rich man will think with his heart,
And surrender a portion of gold.

Tells in the bible, 'Not one sparrow dies',
Without our God knows of its fall,
Tells of a Heaven where all children smile,
Pure paradise for each little soul.

'Everything comes to he who waits',
This is the story I'm told,
'Dear Lord, take the hurting, the babies, their tears,
In Your safe arms of love please enfold.'

As I Grow Older

As I grow older, years rushing past,
My memory harkens back,
To innocent days, gentler ways, when I was but a lass.

Did the summers really last that long?
Did the sun's glow shine brighter then?
Did the snow in winter drift so high?
Or does my mind play tricks again?

Village life was all I knew,
Home from school, run fast,
To farmer's field where Dad was working,
Harvest hay, stacked at last.

Milk was delivered by horse and cart,
By Farmer Rufus and his old mare Phil,
Ladled from churn, to Mum's old jug,
He charged but ½d a gill.

Hand-me-down clothes, make-do, and mend,
Didn't expect anymore,
Ration book living, was all we knew,
Co-op divi, 'Lord's Day' for the poor.

No telly, computer or CDs for us,
All today's 'must have' inventions,
We hadn't been programmed; to buy, buy, buy,
As the young of today are, no question.

Pain

Need to feel my hand in yours,
My father and my lord,
When illness comes into my life,
And pain doth take its toll.

Need You to tell me it's alright,
The pain won't last for long,
Just hold me Saviour when I'm frightened,
Until the hurt has gone.

Need to feel Your arms of love,
Enfold my trembling soul,
Need You to quell the fear inside,
Oh dearest Lord, my all.

No one but You, my loving Jesus,
Understands pain more,
Upon the cross You died for me,
Far greater agony bore.

The nails, the sword, the crown of thorns,
Your suffering had to be,
Death on the cross, the ultimate pain,
You died on the cross for me.

Needed to know you're safe with Father,
Lost in His arms of love,
Needed to know, He healed your pain,
Blessed comforter, God above.

Sadly And Quietly

Affluence abounds in this country we live in,
Want for nothing money can buy,
Every commodity there for the taking,
As in the third world another babe dies.

Cool water, clean filtered from reservoir's bounty,
At the turn of a tap to our homes freshly flows,
Not for the child in the hot arid wasteland,
For the want of a drink, another babe dies.

We take for granted a meal on the table,
'Food mountains' stacked high, so much thrown aside,
Our cups overflowing, girths ever widening,
For the want of a crust, another babe dies.

Wars and famine, rich men and power,
Greed won't listen to a starving boy's cry,
'Dear Lord, help the helpless, show mercy I pray Thee,'
While sadly and quietly, another babe dies.

Dove Of Peace

Oh dove of peace your song is love,
In this world so full of sorrow,
As children cry in pain and fear,
Will there be a bright tomorrow?

Dove of peace, where are you?
Dove of peace come down.

Oh dove of peace where is she now?
In this world where war is spoken,
She hangs her head, her eyes are sad,
She can't fly, her wings are broken.

Dove of peace, where are you?
Dove of peace come down.

Oh dove of peace as children starve,
And war goes on, their food is stolen,
Arms and legs are skin and bone,
Bodies so bloated and swollen.

Dove of peace, where are you?
Dove of peace come down.

Oh Lord of peace please hear the cries,
As young and old lay maimed and dying,
Touch the hearts of evil men,
Turn them to love, instead of fighting.

Dove of peace, where are you?
Lord of peace come down.

Dad's Gift

Can I tell you a story, my hubby tells me,
with a look and a tear in his eye,
it's a tale of a memory from years gone by,
and our magnolia tree,

When the story began,
the tree was a babe,
it was planted with much love and glee,
not knowing the heart thoughts, it was to invoke
when it stood in feet, about three,

'My dad did the planting,' my hubby reports,
and these words he spoke came to be,
'This is something for you when I'm dead and gone
to surely remember me.'

Forty years have gone by,
our magnolia stands tall,
a beauty for all to see, 'Thanks Dad,
for your love, and memories you've left
in our old magnolia tree.'

Jesu's Blanket

Early morn, oh bless'ed day,
Still and newly born,
That such peace could with us stay,
Alas 'twill soon be gone.

Traffic noises start their hurry,
Rend the quiet, all-bustling throng,
People rushing, day's work calling,
Left behind, the peaceful dawn.

Press on through this day God gave us,
Live your dreams, your hopes, your pain,
Careworn day to night surrendered,
'Neath Jesu's blanket, snug again.

The Only Way

Oh come peaceful dove descending,
Spread your wings o'er this hurting land,
End wars heartbreak forever unfolding,
Lord we reap so, just can't understand.

This world is God's own creation,
Such beauty for all to enjoy,
Love's tears are falling like raindrops,
The evil, seem bent to destroy.

When nations speak peace unto nations,
Does man truly mean what he says?
Is the olive branch only a gesture?
Cruelly given, to be stolen away.

Dear Lord, the peaceful are trying,
But man's inhumanity seems to hold sway,
Oh! Salve the tears of the crying,
God's love is the only true way.

Safe Pets

Dear pet lovers, all please heed the call
Keep your dog and cat in tonight,
Behind your closed doors where they are safe,
Whether they're large or small.
November the 5th is fun for our kids
Enjoyed by one and all,
As fires are lit all over our land,
And fireworks whiz and explode,
Oh remember your pets who are trembling in fear
Make sure they are safe indoors
We know our children enjoy this night
Most mums and dads as well,
But remember, remember the 5th of November
To your pet it's a frightening hell.

The Circle

God's love is a circle, pure gossamer threads,
Gentle strength that cannot be broken,
It's made up of hearts who answered His call,
The step of repentance taken,

Come enter God's circle, it widens with love,
Circumference forever increasing,
A mighty throng searching for peace,
The hungry, the lame, the weeping.

Jesus beckons to all, His arms open wide,
For your dear sakes, please answer His call,
Then God's circle of love will encompass the world,
And Satan's regime will fall.

Our Ben

Our old cat had died, and we were sad,
So we went to the kennels to find,
A small dog we thought,
That would be nice,
But what did we buy instead?

Two sad brown eyes looking at us,
Pleading, 'Please take me home.'
He touched out hearts,
So we brought him home,
This pitiful bag of bones,

He was all arms and legs,
With a scar on his head,
He was only a baby, we knew,
What had happened to him, we shudder to think,
But he found us and we brought him home,

Right from the first day he has given us joy,
More than we ever could know,
He's loyal and cheeky,
A comic as well,
He knows how to get his own way,

Tender love shines from those brown eyes now,
Sadness and hurt have all gone,
Long walks he goes with his dad every day,
Up Apple Tree Lane they do go,
A man and his dog, an inseparable pair,
Old Dad sometimes has to go slow,

He waits for the children to come out of school,
As at our gate he sits,
He knows so well as they pass by,
They hug him and give him titbits,
Such love he has given these five years past,
Our collie, our friend, our joy,
Thank God we found him, or did he find us?
Our Ben, our beautiful boy!

Better With Jesus

I feel better when I talk to Jesus,
I feel better when I talk to my Lord,
For I know He's always with me,
If I only listen to His word,

I feel better when I walk with Jesus,
I feel better when I walk with my Lord,
For His steps are always perfect,
And His gentle love assured.

A Cuddle From Jesus

You know that feeling when life gets you down,
And you just can't take anymore,
Problems and battles, troubles and pain,
All the pressures so hard to endure,

You're crying inside where no one can see,
You put on that smile for sure,
To hide the anguish deep within,
Keep it behind your closed door,

But we're not alone, the Lord knows our pain,
Let's talk to Him, He will never leave us,
He knows us all, He loves us all,
So just have a cuddle from Jesus.

Into Autumn

Summer flowers sport their glory,
Pure radiance, nature's wonder-show,
Balmy, sun-kissed, warm and tender,
Evenings share the late sun's glow.

Mature full summer bathed in splendour,
Fruits all ripened on the bough,
To autumn beauty, haze surrendered,
Mellowed brown and golden now.

Grown birds all adorn our garden,
From spring chicks, soft fluffy down,
To feathered, handsome, young and sturdy,
Will next year nurture babes their own.

Crackling wood fires stir the nostrils,
Mist of autumn mingled down,
September evenings fast approaching,
New moon lies in the old moon's arms.

Seasons follow varied season,
Each one with a joy its own,
A treasure of our Lord's bounty,
All nature's gifts, from God alone.

Blackbird

Such a joy to wake at dawn,
Oh bless'ed morn in spring,
And feel my heart and senses stir,
When I hear the blackbird sing,

Pleasure sweet poured o'er my soul,
In every note and trill,
Heralds the new day to come,
His love of life, my heart does fill,

And then once more, when day is done,
He comes to bid goodnight,
With a promise to return next day,
To sing his morning hymn delight.

Story In A Flower

The story of the passion flower,
Was told to me one day,
It touched my heart this lovely ode,
So to you, I would like to convey.

It may be myth, it may be folklore,
I truly cannot say,
But this flower depicts a beautiful story,
The greatest truth that was ever portrayed.

Gaze into the face of this biblical emblem,
And perhaps you'll be overawed,
Three of the nails that pierced His dear flesh,
Five anthers, the wounds of my Lord.

Five fish, five virgins, five foolish ones,
You will also see three loaves,
The apostles, the multitudes, the calyx, the glory,
The pitiful crown of thorns.

The stamens depict the hammers,
That drove cruel nails in His flesh,
Our Lord ministered on Earth for three years,
The flower keeps open three days.

The cross of shame on Calvary's mount,
Hold such an awesome power,
It surely speaks of wonders to me,
When told in the passion flower.

There may be more to this little tale,
I really cannot recall,
But I truly feel, the face of this flower,
Tells the greatest story, of all.

Spring's Promise

Precious season, long-awaited,
Bursting out of winter's gloom,
Buds on Mother trees awakening,
Promises of glory soon.

Daffodils in golden splendour,
Standing sentinel and strong,
Heralds to the wondrous beauty,
Of rainbow flowers yet to come,

Birds are busy, twigs a'finding,
Building homes to rear their young,
Start them out on life's adventures,
Lord, grant them lives both safe and long,

Spring brings about a heartfelt yearning,
New growth, renewal, moving on,
God gives His bounty, never ceasing,
A symphony of nature's song.

Karen Whitehouse

I'm Black-Country born and bred, now living in Tamworth with my husband and two children. I work full-time as a PA to a Partner in a large legal firm in Birmingham City Centre.

My mother introduced me to poetry when I was a baby; I would listen enthralled as she recited a poem each bedtime from a big blue book which had illustrated poems, a different one for every day of the year. I entered my first competition when I was ten with a poem which began, *'When it is my birthday, I am full of glee, all my friends and family come to visit me'.* My friend inspired me to write poetic holiday postcard messages after I received a funny one from her. Upon seeing one of my postcards a colleague asked me to write a poem to celebrate her aunt's 100th birthday and one of the lawyers encouraged me to explore the idea of being commissioned to write bespoke poems after she witnessed me writing one about a colleague having to constantly spell his unusual surname. I have written over 100 poems, many of them bespoke.

I write poetry for pleasure; to give pleasure; to reach out and connect with another person; to make them laugh or make them cry; to let them know I understand; to make them feel special. I also find it cathartic.

I have no specific poetic interest or themes, except the desire to make someone feel special with a personal poem or connect with people through a general poem.

A Weight-Watcher's Lament

For far too long I'd wobbled about,
Unable to stop it all hanging out.
My self-esteem was at an all-time low,
I knew some of this weight just had to go.

So off I wobbled to the Slimming Club,
Feeling like some gigantic tub.
There I met cuddly people who felt the same,
And they helped me play the weighting game.

It's on the scales weekly to see what we've lost,
Knowing if we've cheated it will be to our cost!
After seven tough years I'm three stones light,
Which brings me to my present plight.

Christmas is coming and I'm in a terrible state,
I'm scared I'll put on all that lost weight.
Can I refuse turkey, stuffing and cranberry,
Say 'No!' to the booze but still be merry?

If there is anyone out there who can assist
When temptation proves too hard to resist,
Please get in touch, I'm desperate for advice,
For to indulge without weight would be oh so nice!

My Safety Net

You come across many different people in life,
Some make you happy while some create strife.
Occasionally you're lucky enough to meet a star,
And Sue, my dear friend, that's what you are.

You have sound intuition and it serves you well,
If I put on a brave face, you can always tell.
You help me see things from another perspective,
And that my welfare is your prime objective.

Sensitive towards others with a generous heart,
And that wicked sense of humour sets you apart.
You also inspire others to believe in their ability,
Yet are not afraid to show your own vulnerability.

Yes, we all need a safety net from time to time,
And I'd just like to say, I'm so glad you're mine!

Help Me Help You

(Summing up Britain today)

Help me help you to put 'United' back into our Kingdom,
We all have a role to play to make sure that this gets done!
This land of opportunity has gained a multicultural society,
Our world is getting smaller through advances in technology.

Help me help you to publicise what's good about our country,
We're creative, leaders in fashion, sport, music and film industry.
Our unrivalled voluntary workers run so many different charities.
We have our own distinctive sense of humour and eccentricities!

Help me help you to generate some patriotic pride,
Start by cleaning up our streets, protect the countryside.
Each and every one of us is unique, which should be respected,
Our differences must not be mocked, ridiculed or rejected.

Help me help you to face change, embrace change, lead the way,
Kingdom might be old-fashioned, but we're a country of today.
Come on pull together, let's be the masters of our country's fate,
United Kingdom was and, with our help, can once again be Great!

Bombs Away

It was the silent dead of night,
When I suddenly woke up in a fright.
A big angry fly dive-bombed my head,
Causing me to leap out of bed.

I switched on the light to entice it away,
Slamming the door to keep it at bay,
I was just nodding off to its distant hum,
The buzzing grew louder - there was more to come!

It had snook under the door,
To dive-bomb me once more!
A Stephen King nightmare making me quake,
Not to mention keeping me awake.

Fortunately my knight in shining armour,
Helped me begin to feel calmer,
By coming to my rescue,
Opened the window and out the beast flew!

The Secretaries' Lament

Old-fashioned values don't count anymore,
Hard work and effort gets you labelled a bore.
Keeping good time and working each day,
No appreciation, just, 'How long can you stay?'

To churn it all out you work through your break,
But all that's remembered is a typing mistake.
'Hello, how's your partner, kids, cat or home?'
Don't bother to answer, it's to someone on the phone!

Eyes red from perpetually staring at the screen,
Headaches deciphering what the squiggles mean.
Across the floor, the 'phones ring all of the time,
What a nightmare, I can only pick up mine!

'Stop what you're doing, do this straightaway.'
'Isn't that done yet? It's been with you all day!'
Between copier and fax you race around the room,
Yes, all that's missing is the proverbial broom!

Although we're way down in the pecking line,
If we're not around, listen to the bosses whine.
And we know we get paid for the work that we do,
But we're also people who need to feel valued too.

So when you foreclose that lucrative deal,
Take a little time to think how we feel.
Because, let's face it, at the end of the day,
We all have an important role to play!

Redundancy

The holidays are over and Christmas is looming,
Fingers crossed, the economy will be booming.
So much to buy, the shops will be heaving,
But don't look to us because we're all leaving.

A parting of the ways has been forced upon us,
It was inevitable, so pointless kicking up a fuss.
Yes, sadly, it's been on the cards for a while,
So stiff upper lip and paint on that smile.

Alas, a life of leisure is not written in the stars,
Perhaps there's work going on the planet Mars!
Whatever fate has in store - I'm afraid this is it,
And frankly, my dears, we don't give a . . . damn!

Nobody Holds On Anymore

There is so much, perhaps too much, available today,
If you don't like something, you just chuck it away.
Nothing seems to matter, what's it all for?
    Nobody holds on anymore

Indeed, so many of us are spoilt for choice now,
It seems that our values have been diluted somehow.
'What's that you say? Make do? Don't be a bore.'
    Nobody holds on anymore.

It's not my fault; I've done it, but don't look at me,
Because my actions are someone else's responsibility,
I'm certainly not answerable, that's for sure.
    Nobody holds on anymore.

Instant gratification can leave us spiritually bereft,
So often dissatisfied with what we have left,
Yet we buy more cos, that's what money's for.
    Nobody holds on anymore.

Why bother? What's the point? Who cares?
Why get married? Just have lots of affairs.
Who needs kids, the expense leaves you poor.
    Nobody holds on anymore.

But be aware my friend, please take heed,
There might come a time when you're in need,
For you only get back from life what you put in,
So might end up with the rubbish - thrown in the bin,
Discarded, trampled on, shaken to the core!
Because let's face it, nobody holds on anymore!

Wedded Bliss

You've bought the ring and tied the knot,
Caved under pressure, accepted your lot,
Kissed goodbye to your bachelor days,
Those carefree memories now a distant haze!

There'll be no more doing just as you please,
Because now there's someone else to appease!
With fewer boys' nights downing the booze,
By now you must be thinking, 'What else can I lose?'

Well I'm sorry to tell you there's more to come,
Now rumour has it that you're under the thumb!
But before you throw up your hands in despair,
Feel sorry for yourself, that life's so unfair . . .

Take heart, it's my guess that, just like you,
Your mates will soon be taking the plunge too!
And they'll also be enjoying wedded bliss,
Thus preventing them taking the proverbial . . .

Yellow Peril

Who is that chap in the canary yellow shirt?
Pass my sunglasses, my eyes are starting to hurt.
Do you reckon he's trying to make a statement?
If we asked him to remove it, would he consent?
Maybe he's really hoping we'll kick up a fuss,
Because secretly he'd like to do a strip for us!
Perhaps he'd like to chuck his contracts away,
And longs to join the Chippendales one day!
Could it be he finds his job too boring by half?
So wears something outrageous to raise a laff!
Well one thing's for sure, he's certainly made us titter!
What's that you say? He's got one covered in *glitter!*

It's Good To Talk

There will be various periods throughout your life,
When all you encounter is trouble and strife.
People and circumstances get you down,
Your smile will be replaced by a woeful frown.

With self-esteem rock bottom you'll feel all alone,
Resilience gone, you'll just want to wail and moan.
Unhappiness and sorrow seem all you have left,
Joy and enthusiasm gone and you'll feel bereft.

At times like this family and friends are not enough,
For you to cope when the going gets tough.
But take heart for there is one more avenue,
A voice on the 'phone to listen and advise you.

You can pour out your troubles, say how you feel,
Be reassured you're not silly, your problems are real.
With care and consideration a solution can be reached,
And you can be confident your trust will not be breached.

To help a sad person put things in perspective,
Make them feel their welfare is your prime objective,
To know you can reach out, comfort and console,
Is to be a counsellor - a very rewarding and vital role.

Ways To Make More Time

Your time is very precious so use it well,
Plan beforehand and the results will tell.
By starting with a list of tasks to be done,
Your battle for time is already half won.

Do be realistic in your own expectations,
Otherwise it will affect working relations.
If it's not your work and you haven't time
Learn to say, 'No, I'm working on mine.'

Decide who you're on call to, that's the test,
Then get someone else to deal with the rest.
Be ruthless with time and gracious with folk,
Or else your routine will be an ongoing joke.

Use other people's offices to discuss any stuff,
It's easier to escape when you've had enough.
Finish one job before moving on to the next,
Otherwise you'll end up frustrated and vexed.

Telephone interruptions can be an energy drain,
They reduce efficiency and are an irksome pain.
Take control, divert or voicemail, that's the style,
And let someone else take your calls for a while.

We all need a little stress to get the best from us,
A shot of adrenaline, to get that enthusiastic buzz.
Recognise the difference between stress and strife,
Create a balance and see the funny side of life.

Dream Garden

A room with a view, is all I desire,
A garden of splendour, for all to admire.
Luscious lawns and fruit-filled trees,
Ornamental grasses blowing in the breeze.
Cascading water and a fish-filled pond,
A family of ducks of which to grow fond.
To watch the birds taking their daily bread,
While squirrels scamper on the potting shed.
To follow the butterflies floating along,
In the peace and quiet of nature's own song.
The season's flowers and hedgerow housing nest,
Give me the grounds and I promise to do the rest.

Requiem For An Old Pal

Adorable Matthew, my most loyal and open companion,
Has passed away peacefully. He has gone.
Courageous until the very end,
Oh, how I will miss my little friend.

No longer will I hear his paws,
Echo across the wooden floors.
No longer will I hear his reassuring bark,
See his smiling eyes, concerned, affectionate, so dark.

I'm reminded of him at every turn, he is everywhere,
His clothes, his bowl, his favourite chair.
He possessed beauty without insolence, vice or ferocity.
He was my canine friend, very special to me.

You and I could learn a valuable lesson or two,
Tolerance, acceptance, devotion, unconditional love, are a few.
Goodnight sweet prince, flights of angels sing thee to thy rest,
You were my friend, my life, you were simply the best.

Extreme Measures

(Sinéad, a newly appointed law lecturer and Richard, a surgeon, had a terrible accident in France, their bicycles collided and Sinéad's face was badly smashed.)

I hope you don't mind Sinéad,
But Dawn has told me of your French escapade.
Tell me, does your new career,
Fill Richard with fear?
Is he really concerned,
That his advances will be spurned?
That you will prefer a student for new pleasures,
And so he has resorted to extreme measures!
In order to keep ahead of the race,
Has he decided to smash up your face?
Or is he branching out into plastic surgery,
And wants someone to work on for free!
Sorry couldn't resist poking fun,
I truly hope no lasting harm is done.
And poor Richard must be absolutely distraught,
Hey - take a photo for the grandkids - now there's a thought!

Hair-Raising

From beginning to end, no two days are the same,
There are tresses to tease and wild locks to tame.
Working hours to suit and skills to use anywhere,
It's a job for life, machines can't do people's hair.

There's cutting and colouring, plaiting and pleating,
Highlights and lowlights, crimping and treating.
Blow-drying and styling, shaving and lengthening.
Waxing and perming, straightening and strengthening.

Different people to meet, new friendships to be made,
Old problems to be shared and new ideas to trade.
Regular clients are like family, part of our daily life,
We become agony aunts while listening to their strife.

We make the job seem easy, but it's hard on our feet,
And customers' needs must be met before we can eat.
Remember we have feelings and a necessary job to do,
Be honest, you probably need us more than we need you!

Change

I like change,
To rearrange.
To try a different angle,
See what I can wangle.

Check if there's a better way,
To spend the hours of my day.
Always looking to improve,
Then maybe make a move.

I embrace change,
Which might sound strange,
To those of us more content,
With how their lot is spent.

Claire A J Veitch

The poetry I write has been a recent journey for me. I started writing after being ill for a number of months.

My poems range from hospital themes right through to nature, the sea, animals and everyday life. They actually just pop into my head and I simply write them down, mostly without too much 'tweaking'.

I have always lived in Suffolk and have been married for 24 years and I have two teenage sons and four cats.

I enjoy gardening and all the challenges it brings. I am very much inspired by things and people around me.

Sandcastles

Dig, dig, dig, the spade works quickly,
digging deeper for the treasure.
Sandy coves and castles high,
make a spectacular sight.

Buckets ready to fill,
all lined up to attention.
Bright colours,
all shapes and sizes.

Castles appear along the shore,
ready to be claimed by the sea.
Works of art decorated with flags,
pretty stones and shells.

But by tomorrow it will all be gone.

Hospitals

Hot and dry,
draughty in the corridors.

Beds, three in a row,
wheels at the ready.

Up and down they go,
but all have a brake!

Some have a special mattress,
pillows piled high, sometimes five.

Nurses' trolleys whizzing around,
the drugs' trolley.

The OBS trolley,
and the dirty linen trolley.

Cleaning ladies clatter around,
with broom, mop and bucket.

Sometimes a cloth,
and with fresh water too.

Three meals a day,
porridge for breakfast, really quite nice.

Choices for lunch and supper,
served on a tray at your bed.

Hospitals - a little like hotels,
but with lots of wheels.

Visitors

Full of cheer, bearing gifts,
lots to tell, full of news.

Sometimes two, sometimes four,
never enough chairs to perch on.

Talking quietly, sometimes laughing,
bringing news from the outside world.

Sit near the bed, sometimes on it,
listening intently to the patients.

Visiting time 3pm - 8pm,
maybe a few, or they fill the ward.

A comfort for patients,
to see a familiar face.

Amidst the daily routine,
of the hospital and its staff.

The Gardens, Papworth

Lawned walkways,
daisies in the grass.

Trees and bushes,
all shades of green, purple and brown.

Gently swaying, and whispering in the breeze.

Wooden benches scattered and hidden,
perfect sun traps waiting to be found.

Birds singing high in the trees,
and rustling in the undergrowth.

A faint cry of children's voices
playing in the sunshine.

Wood pigeons cooing,
and a wasp flies by.

A boiling shimmering hot day,
to enjoy the scenery.

Cats

Purring, singing, growling,
cats do all these things.

Sometimes playful, sometimes moody,
sometimes awake, sometimes asleep.

Catching prey, catching the rays,
cats take their pick on sunny days.

Some friendly and mellow,
others aloof and distant.

Miaowing for food, some also sing,
get under your feet, pestering around.

Different breeds, all colours and sizes.
Some would say, a 'purrfect' pet!

Cats II

Big cats, small cats,
fat cats, thin cats.

Cats that purr,
cats that hiss.

Clean cats, wet cats,
sleepy cats, lively cats.

Cats that eat,
cats that drink.

Stripy cats, spotty cats,
black cats, white cats.

Cats that hunt,
cats that don't.

All kind of cats.

Cats Again

Licking and preening,
purring and buzzing.

Dozing in the sun,
on the best soft chair.

Twitching in sleep,
dreaming of the big catch.

Awoken by noise -
ah well, time for lunch.

Swimming In The Garden

Splashing, squealing, laughing,
jumping in and out, slipping around.

Under the waves, above the water,
gentle waves lapping the edges.

Distant music, sunny afternoon, warm breeze,
gurgling noises, floating and sculling along.

'Watch me, Dad, I'm swimming.'
Dad looks on and smiles at the child.

Empty pool, cool evening breeze,
silence in the garden, more swimming
tomorrow.

Mum

Always there, never judging
Smiling face, radiating love

Hugging us all
Hugging the world

Bright shining person
Wise and calm

Loving the animals
Plants and life

Teamwork we used
Always together

Strong with her love
Strong like the trees

Witty with words
Stories to tell

Beautiful life
Beautiful Mum.

Dad

Strong and kind
Clever and calm

Making and mending
Building and painting

Laughter and tears
Talking was fun

Childhood memories
All seasons through

Special times
Special Dad

Sisters

Sisters are strong
Sisters are fun

Sisters are one
Sisters are two

Sisters do
Sisters act

Sisters laugh
Sisters cry

Sisters hug
Sisters love

Sisters are forever
Sisters are fact

Peace

Peace in the trees
peace on the ground.

Peace in the air
peace all around.

Peace with the flowers
peace in the meadows.

Peace in the shade
peace in the sun.

Peace in the stillness
peace in the quiet.

Peace in the grass
peace on the land.

Peace in the cemetery.

Grief

It comes and goes
Wells up and engulfs you.
Creeps along and takes a hold
Then slips away, lurking, waiting.

Some days, too much pain
Burning, crying, panic and darkness.
Looking in from the outside
Talking but no one hears.

Head in turmoil
Spinning, whirring in overdrive.
Thoughts sloshing around
Please put them in their boxes.

How to face the world
Pretend with a smile.
Tell them you're OK
They don't get it, do they?

Calmness and poise return
Slipping back into real time for a while.
Think about pending errands
Shut out the pain, at least for now.

Grief is real and always around
Ready to pounce and threaten the mind.
Fond memories return to comfort
Try to keep balanced and cope if you dare!

Egypt

Vast sugary bowl of custard
Sprinkled with granules of glass.
Shimmering into the distance
Distorted by heat and tricks of the eye.

Camels lolloping into the dunes
Snort and spit to show their disgust.
Commands of children slow the beasts
At journey's end they rest and feed.

Sizzling sun and azure blue skies
Egypt knows no clouds.
Scorching temples bold and erect
Fusty smells and dusty trails.

Uneven steps, worn and faded
Yet still strong and sound.
Gigantic columns of open and closed papyrus flowers
Buried for centuries under the sands.

Beautiful encryptions of historical fact
Stand to attention for closer scrutiny.
Egyptian pharaohs and their queens
With kings and princes adorn the walls.

Gently gliding along the riverbank
Oxen bathe with heron and children.
Muddy waters displaced with care
Then the tea bell rings to summon the guests.

The street sellers banter and thrust their wares.
Tourists laugh and some seem shy.
Clattering carriages fill the streets
With honking cars and vans alike.

Mind the potholes and where's the path?
Keep together and find a retreat.
Luxor's temple serene and quiet
Yet 1000s of footsteps pound the way.

Sights to behold and are they real?
Baby alligators, snakes and lambs.
Barefoot children smile and chatter
Before descending with goods and chattels.

Beautiful Egypt, glorious and hot
Never-ending stories, passageways and delight.
Wondrous sights stretching into the sky
First time I've been, have just started the journey.

Tennis And All That!

The thud on the sweet spot
Balls zing past.
Player flounders
The striker rejoices.

The ace served so perfect
Another point won.
That felt good
Must do it again.

Strawberries and cream
A glass of champagne.
Shall we have seconds
Or is that not done?

The grunting of players
As they strike the ball.
Passing shots, volleys
Rallies and smashes.

The towelling down
To disperse the sweat.
Change of ends
Only 90 seconds allowed.

Take on a drink
Maybe water or squash.
Hurry along now
Umpire is ready for play.

The crowd roars and claps
To behold the play
Some are dozing
Others are enthralled.

The end of the match
Players shake hands.
The court erupts
The players take a bow.

Down comes the net
Let's call it a day.
Out pops the mower
To trim up the grass.

The crowds wander home
Happy with their snaps.
We must come again
Too much to take in.

Lizzie Cooper

I was born on the 24th December 1990. I am originally from Leicester then moved to Whitby four years ago with my parents and three brothers. I am currently in year 9 at Eskdale school in Whitby.

I write poetry because I see it as a way of letting out and expressing your emotions whether it's happy or sad; also it's a good way of showing people what you are, even though your vision and opinion on a poem may have a different effect or meaning to everyone else.

When I write poetry, anything can inspire me, but staring out of my bedroom window for a while helps; a lot of things influence me like the habits people have or the way things move, but some of my favourite poets such as Roger McGough, Peter Dixon and Mike Jubb always inspire me by their poetry.

Most of the time I just think of a word and then see what happens! Another thing that influences me is the TV. Right now I've just had an inspiration for a poem about school.

I like lots of things such as music and drama, where some of my poems come from. Also I study German which I enjoy a lot. But of course I enjoy poetry and have entered a few competitions to get recognised as a poet.

Recurrent themes in my poetry don't often happen one after another but all on different subjects and then I might have an idea for a theme I've already written about. I enjoy writing both nonsense and real-life poems because they're at both ends of the scale and it usually helps in writing poems on other themes.

What I Saw

Her naked child sat on the roadside
Begging for nothing

All she has is there before you
But all she has, she gives to her child

They live with hate, poverty and rejection
That is all they know

But there's nothing I can do
So how do I live, knowing that?

How do you live, knowing that?
Maybe there's nothing you want to do.

Time

Seconds flash by,
Minutes carry on,
Hours walk by,
Days move on.

Weeks flutter by,
Months plod on,
Years go by,
Centuries creep on.

War

They think it solves everything,
blowing up anyone or anything.

Scheming to get revenge,
and not caring if their life ends.

Hurting the innocent,
killing the young, the rich and the poor.

All they needed was a simple apology,
because how hard is it to say that you're sorry?

?

When you look at your secret dreams
What do you see?

When you look into the deep ocean
What do you see?

When you look at the endless stars
What do you see?

Odd Landmarks

The pink cliffs of Dover
Sat on the edge
A nice sort of pink though
Sat on the edge.

The great road of China
Miles and miles
Very, very big
And can be seen from outer space.

The London Nose
Very, very round
You can even ride in it
Going up and down.

The East Pole
Sticking out in red and white
Not easy to miss
Though it's hard to find.

Rainbow

R eally
A wesome
I ngeniously
N ice
B eautifully
O bviously
W onderful.

That is a rainbow
After the storm.

Best Mates

Me and my best mate
Walk to school together
So why are we always late?
We go to each other's for tea
Fish fingers, chips and beans
We play at the local park
And always have a laugh
Every weekend we have a sleepover
Staying up all night
Watching our favourite films
Eating popcorn and Angel Delight
All over the summer
We mess about having fun
But when school starts again
Guess what? We're always late!
Me and my best mate.

Music

From pop to opera,
Saxophone to flute,
There's always music
For everyone.

Hard rock, punk, house, garage,
Classical, blues, jazz and R&B
Golden oldies, one-hit wonders,
Cheesy pop bands and 'great hits'.

If you look hard enough
You'll find music you like
Because there's music for everyone
There's always music.

The 'B' Word

I've tried and tried and tried
I can't find anything to do
I've tried board games and the park
Even polishing my mum's shoes
I've watched the news and tidied my room
Even doing my homework
My mates say I'm doomed!
I give up! I'm bored
But now I'm going
I'm going to write a poem.

After They've Gone

It's 4pm now,
The tourists have all gone,
Leaving the town in a mess,
Doggy-doo-doos, chocolate wrappers,
Even the odd lolly stick.

Why didn't they tidy their mess?
Instead they left it for us,
Maybe we should go to their town,
Mess it up for them to tidy,
After we've gone.

Summer

School's out for summer
Yippee! Hooray!
School's out for summer
Yahoo! Hey-hey!

Playing in the garden
Hanging out at the park
Eating millions of ice cream
Wahoo! What a laugh!

Throwing slumber parties
Watching cool films
Having fun camping out
And sliding down big hills!

Staying up late
Watching loads of TV
Having long lie-ins
That's summer for me.

The Celebrity

Walking around,
Crowded by fans,
Asking for autographs,
With bodyguards around,
Winning awards,
In fancy costumes,
Down the red carpet,
Out of big limos,
Going out shopping,
Hunted by the press,
Reported in newspapers.
Criticised on the way they dress,
Watched on the TV,
On posters on our walls,
And loved by all.

The Lonely Café

The lonely café
At the end of the high street
Next to the chemist
Only it doesn't sell anything to eat.

The lonely café
Only used by passers-by
Lugging their shopping
Wishing for apple pie.

The lonely café
Small cosy and kinda sweet
But you see
There's nothing good to eat!

The Secret Life Of Our Undercover Teachers

Our teacher isn't really a teacher
She's really a spy working undercover for MI5
And this job is just a cover-up
Because really the head's a master villain
Obviously to hide his master plan to take over the world
And he's taken the science and French teachers hostage
Of course they're being guarded by the maths teacher
The head's evil sidekick
But now our teacher has a plan
To foil the head's evil plot and save the world
She snook around the back of the kitchens
Which the head had taken over
(Being a master villain can be hungry work, you know)
She slid through an open window
And saw last week's mouldy leftovers in the bin
She grabbed it and crept up on the head
Shoved it all over him and his evil white cat
Then karate-kicked the maths teacher
After that she freed the hostages
And then a pink sports car turned up
And our teacher drove off into the sunset
So everyone lived happily ever after
Apart from the three mouldy leftover-covered villains
Who rotted together in a maximum security prison
Our head, the maths teacher and the evil white cat.

The Last

The last loser of the last race
The last minute of the last game
The last time you tidied your room
The last time a bully called you a name

The last day of the last school year
The last word of the last book you read
The last second you are asleep
The last thing you ever said

The last day of the last year
The last time you were ever kind
The last bullet of the last war
And this is the last line!

Gillian Maynard

I was born on 27th October 1951 in Ponders End, Enfield. A working class background and attended a secondary modern girls school. I have four children ranging from 21-35 years old and two grandchildren. Divorced, I have lived with my partner for 9 years in Edmonton, North London until we decided to move to Hastings Old Town during the summer of 2003. We actually moved in October.

A spiritualist at heart and have sat in circles to develop my awareness. I wrote 'Titanic' because I have a spiritual guide who was an officer on the ship, he is my 'battery booster'. I wrote 'Slow Decline' a week before I moved from London, overcome with mixed feelings of sadness and anger at the way young human beings are becoming violent and unruly.

My inspiration comes from life, my loves, my loses and everyday situations. I have never attended poetry groups or had any training. My work has been taken into the classroom and read out to 17-19 year old students who have gone back to school for one reason or another. The poetry lesson was a complete success. The teenagers were amazed that a grandmother, now working as a care assistant could write material that youngsters could relate to and enjoy. Anything can trigger my inspiration, an article in a newspaper or a TV programme. I have been asked to go into the classroom and help the teacher 'teach' poetry writing. I am very busy working, but I would love one day, to devote more time to my writing. I get great satisfaction when the words start flowing and form a poetic story and hope one day to have a big enough collection to publish my own book, so that others can enjoy the poems. I was told that in the classroom, my poems prompted good discussions, which can't be bad.

The Final Drink

After a hard week's graft
The men walked to the pub
Building up an appetite
For their Sunday lunchtime grub
Suddenly they came
Flying not much higher than the waves
People ran for cover
Hiding in the Hastings caves
Bombs started falling
Killing rich and poor
The pub with the men in
Now stands no more
We remember the stench
We remember the fear
We'll always remember the men
Having their Sunday lunchtime beer.

Slow Decline

I live in London
It is no fun
People are warming to the sound of the gun.
The knife is becoming old hat seems to me,
I'm leaving London for the sound of the sea.
Lawless streets, kids on the make,
Whose house next do they decide to break.
Do what they like - get to slap,
No respect, when on crack.
No discipline, no rules, no clout from the cop,
I now wonder if and when it's going to stop.
Adults are nothing it's the kids that rule,
Shame the kids don't appreciate school.
Shame their brains are wasting away
Smoking pot and crack all day.
Hooded up they go a walking
Down the alleyways they go a stalking.
Easy prey, they're looking for,
Walk along - what door? What door?
Little old lady now fights for her life.
Gun toting kids - yeah, they're rife!

Rubbish

Rubbish put in bin bags
Broken open by the cats.
A nice nutritional meal
For the ugly hunched back rats.

Chicken bones, takeaways
Leftovers of Sunday brunch.
Foxes prowl down our streets
Looking for a tasty lunch.

Bags split open -
Rubbish spills in disarray.
As it blows along our streets
What does the council say?

Why can't we go back to the good old days?
When the rubbish stayed in the bin
Until the workmen came around
And took what was within.

Nice Meal Dear?

We're going for a meal tonight -
Knightsbridge, that's the place.
Jump into the Mercedes
The traffic to embrace.
Lobster or steak, fillet of lamb
The choice is yours, my dear.
Glass of wine,
Champagne is fine
Or a nice cold glass of beer?

In they bound, doors flung wide
Shining axes by their sides.
A baseball bat one does hold
Standing there, oh so bold.
Arms they rise, weapons held high,
Demanding jewellery or men will die.
Fill their bags with gold and cash
Then out the door they do dash.

Violence is disturbing
It affects the soul and mind.
Do we have to put up with
Human beings of this kind?

The women they cry
And the men feel sad.
The world is very scary
And the world is going mad.

When Our Paths Crossed

We met along a pathway,
We stopped to say hello.
We felt we liked each other,
So our love began to flow.

I don't say I'm perfect,
I have my faults for sure.
But I care about you dearly,
And I want you more and more.

I didn't mean to hurt you,
I don't want to say goodbye.
For if we do, our paths may not meet again
Until the day we die.

What a shame to lose the love we have
For the sake of foolish pride.
Let's find a little forgiveness
In these hearts we try to hide!

Natter Natter

Oh, by the way,
I haven't had ten men between Rod and Dean,
Perhaps one or two were quite serious.
Three or four knocked at the door -
Now and then,
But I wasn't head spun delirious!

You know,
I should have taken pen to paper years ago.
I could have been a writer, a printer of words,
Instead I wasted life and mixed with a lot of nerds!
Oh, I mustn't complain, I suppose,
I have four kids to my credit.
Although, they do drain one dry
And they smile, rather sly
When the bank balance shows debit, debit, debit.

How's your man, is he back from Toronto?
And did he ever buy that Fiat Punto?
And was it true
He made love to Sue
Down in Father Christmas' grotto?

Oh, don't cry and fret!
He'll be back with goodies and jewels to befriend you!
But just keep one eye open,
For girls with love potions,
Because there are one or two that would do!

Dreams

In our dreams we drift away
Reliving events of a far nicer day.
Premonitions fill our head,
Visitations whilst in our bed.
Weird and wonderful, the future unfolds
Sometimes frightening stories to be told.
Where do they come from, these obscure thoughts?
Where do they come from indeed.
Where and who is the powerful one
That carefully sows the seed?
Relax and listen, he'll talk to you
The same as he talks to me.
Unwind, dream on and drift away
Then one day, *you* will see.

New Love

Summer evenings are fading
Winter nights are drawing near.
Your arms so snug around me
The loss of your love I fear.

The fire in my heart is glowing
This feeling is soon bound to show.
Fingers touching, lips are quivering
I'm sure they will all soon know.

I want you in the morning,
I need you late at night.
Surround me with love adorning,
It can't be wrong when it feels so right.

Sleep Tight Darling

Doors flung open in the middle of the night,
Give us your car keys or we'll give you a fight.
Men in balaclavas, their faces they hide.
Privacy and safety are on a deep slide.
Give us your Saab or the four wheel drive;
Hard earned cash off you, they'll deprive.
What's the point? I might as well give in.
Punch them on the nose! Oh no - that's a sin.
Law and order is on the decline,
Gone are days when my assets are mine.
Don't feel safe in my bed anymore
In case balaclava men come banging on the door.

Across The Miles

Miles apart, I miss you.
Morning breaks, I want to kiss you.
Shall we ever see the dawn,
Feel the dew on misty morns?
Flowers opening,
Shadows forming,
I miss you.

Letting Go

The ache in my heart has now gone
The love we once knew is no more
I am now where I belong
In the arms of a new love, for sure

The distance between us grows each day
The memories we shared are fading
The pain which caused my body to cry
Drifts with the breeze in the morning.

'Twas love - yes love that helped me through
And faith in a power unseen
A guiding light, a ray from above
A message received in a dream.

The Pathway Of Life

We walk along the path of life
Sometimes many roads to choose.
Our burdens getting heavy -
We can hardly move.

Please take this weight from me,
For this I cannot bear.
Help me, bright light,
For I know you really care.

Guide me gently as I go
Help me to decide,
Which way to walk
Which path to tread, my trust in you I bestow.

I cling to you so closely
I dare not close my eyes.
The crossroads of life are many,
Help me to be *extra* wise!

Love You Dad

I remember the picnics
I remember the fun
I remember the days
When you used to help Mum
The caravan holidays
The days by the sea
Going to Aunt Till's
For a lovely Sunday tea
As I grew older
With children by my side
Out we would go again
For a pleasant country ride
Suddenly you left me
Your life came to an end
But I know you're looking down on me
And I know your love you send
I think of you fondly
Every minute of the day
'I love you Dad'
That's all I want to say.

For The Children

The days were long when I was young
Relatively safe and full of fun.
Parks and woods were ours to explore,
Free to roam, nature to adore.
Trees to climb, rivers to swim
Trails to walk, caves to hide in.
Now mothers watch their children grow
Amidst the horror of what's on show.
Show us your knickers; I'll give you a penny
Paedophiles - there are too many.
Come home with me, I'll give you a sweet.
Little do they know - that won't be the treat.
Listen up children, the adults are sick
Watching young girls perform the next trick.
Watch your backs when you go out to play
And I'll just pray for a far safer day.

The Forgotten Children

Little children lay so helpless,
Abandoned in a world uncaring.
Tiny eyes and lips uncherished,
Bodies that long for a mother's embrace.

Days that seem so utterly endless.
Thrashing limbs against the rails.
Minds that rot for failure of learning
Spirit departs - and up it sails -
To better ways - happier days.
Don't forget them -
The children of Romania.

Titanic

Ice-cold seas surround us,
The stars are shining bright.
Our hope is slowly fading
Into the still of the night.

'Launch the lifeboats,' the captain calls,
'Women and children go first.'
Husbands and fathers left behind
To their fate - yet unrehearsed.

Let's not forget these poor souls
A chance they did not stand.
Cold seas rush up around them
Nearer my God to thee - played the band.

Hours are now numbered and
Death is drawing near.
'Don't forget me, I'm now gone
From this world I loved so dear.'

Do We Listen

The planet is dying
Mother Nature's hitting back.
It's time for the human race
To be placed upon the rack.

Great floods and ice are on their way,
The Gulf Stream slows, day by day.
The future of the Earth I do dread,
For I fear we'll all, soon be dead.

The planet is dying.
Do we listen?
Do we care?

The planet is dying
Do we listen?

Do we dare!

John Rafferty

Why do I write poems? Is it because I have always read poems, because I've loved literature for as long as I can remember? It's only natural to wish to emulate people you admire: the difficulty is in avoiding the temptation to imitate, without looking into yourself and at the world around you.

I have an abiding interest in history, and this has affected the way I write, as well as providing several themes. Even when I have written short stories, they are poems trying to break through. My favourite author is not a poet at all. I revere him as a writer and as a human being. For me, Chekhov has that fusion of gloom and humour which is moving and inspirational. I can't begin to list the poets I treasure. Like composers, some are in and out of fashion, but not in my book.

Although born in the Midlands, I have spent most of my life in the North. I won a prize in the Manchester Poets open competition in 1997, and a commendation two years later. Having to read in front of an audience was not something that came easily to me. Essentially, I'm a private person. Acquaintances urge me to come out of my shell. One said, 'You sell yourself by not selling yourself.' He was a salesman.

Why do I write poems? I have absolutely no idea.

Fast And Loose

Korolenko wrote a story called *The Murmuring*
Forest, full of menace as well as enchantment.

As urban children we were taken to the woods
for a treat. Bluebells and wild garlic, with clearings

where a prehistoric bird might land: leathery
pterodactyl, toothy archaeopteryx.

Chris is adamant one or the other removed
the golden carp from her garden pond, promises

to keep vigil with a shotgun while her quaking
dog and cat curl up alongside Prozac, the blind

hamster. The fishermen back her up, protesting
these monsters have had the effrontery to seize

their barracuda. Most people are sceptical,
listening to such claims. Writhing Isaac has tiny

black eyes and can imagine his wife's belly scar
being down to an other-world experience, rather

than a routine piece of surgery. A golf ball
in the undergrowth and all the dead echoes of

fore. So, where did that come from? Consideration
of several possibilities: an overhit

drive, a pull or slice, made worse by an infernal
crosswind, pinballing from tree to tree, or a man

taking a short cut, with a hole in his bucket,
making his living selling them back to the club.

What, buckets? We stare disdainfully, aware that
she is the youngest but making no allowance.

I do not tell my dad that here someone tried to
molest me. I do not understand the meaning

of *molest*. I tell no one about it for all
of thirty-five years and, in that time, never think

of it once. I get away by agreeing to
come back the following day, having no intention

of keeping my word. Learning at a delicate age
the value, and the necessity, of telling lies.

His Own Face

More than sixty, far and wide: executions.
Stared-at and disintegrating mirrors
reconstituted as The Slaughtered Ox.

Hung up like humanity on a gallows
of thick oak, imitated by Delacroix
and Soutine, who saw more than a carcass,

more than meat, though the cannibals prevail.
His defiance, above ruff and plate armour:
with wispy moustache under a broad nose.

His resignation, marked forehead and lost eyes.
A subject, a creature of flesh and blood,
it's true, but with quite another dimension.

This miller's son, out of Leyden, not spoiled,
not even floored by insatiable entrepreneurs
and evangelists, and vile dukes of Alba.

Fireweed

Wherever woodland is cleared in one war,
wherever air raids cause devastation
in another: in any area of wasteland

here is rosebay willowherb with its plumes
of seeds and its habit of taking over,
like waving fans of ferns above heather.

Taking over quarries and canal banks,
picked in armfuls by fascinated children
who didn't realise their hands were black

from the accumulated soot. Terraces
of mothers wondering what they had done
to deserve this latest addition to

the cost of keeping them clean. They climb
trees and end up looking like miners,
holding a few speckled birds eggs, hiding

them under those giant rhubarb-like plants
where you could make a den and shelter,
stand up and see a mass of colour

which was magical, caught on your clothes
like weft. Daring to drink by the lock gates,
racing away from broken windows,

stolen candyfloss and drowned goldfish:
toffee apples with their sickening sour
centre and grown men trying to break open

coconuts by stamping their boots before
the whole sorry episode became a game
of football with no rules and no referee.

Most Unlikely

Tortoiseshell was his name: he bore it
like a double chin. He looked older
than the teachers and leapfrogged
into his father's law firm, hangdog
expression suited to particular cases.

He languished after Miss Pickering,
who kept herself to herself. This state
of affairs obtained for several years:
why not accost her and observe
we're neither of us getting any younger.
But no. Another eternity went by.

There was a rumour her parents
had been spiritualists: he would listen
to rumour. On his fortieth birthday, or
was it his forty-first, not knowing
where the words came from, he said

would she care for a quick one
in the Daisyfield. It's nice in here,
she said, look they still have service
buttons. Though nothing happened
when they dared to press. How long
had they known one another, he said:

she wondered was there something
he wanted to ask. He said yes,
and asked her what time it was,
if she had the time, whether there
was time, and so on, till time was called.

She went to meet her Redeemer,
and he was found to have been playing
fast and loose with clients' accounts.
In prison he had that same perplexed
appearance he had in the corridors
at school or, worst of all, on sports day.

A Single Daffodil

Nothing much. Lying by the kerb,
kicked there by someone angry
at something, or perhaps without
feelings at all, unless opposed
to all the colours bursting through

in the face of forecasts of doom
which have their reassuring side.
Placed in a bottle retrieved from
the undergrowth of a garden
skimmed over by mechanical

contrivances and left alone
by old-fashioned rakes, finally
cleaned up to reveal a raised base
and narrow neck suitable
for the stem of one vandalised

flower or one spill of incense
to smoulder away its perfume
like the ruined furnace of old plant.
Soft ore everywhere, you only
have to open your eyes, apply

your sensitivity, your sense
of touch to this imitation
lunar surface with features grey
enough to include open-cast
mining, derailments of limestone,

fractured gas mains, water hissing
up at you even in periods
of drought. So this yellow trumpet
heralds nothing much: patently
it is going to make no difference

to those entrances and exits
worn like insignias principally
for pecking-order recognition.
Here is a dying thing, its line
dislocated by liquid and glass.

From The Fells To The Coast

Never mind the cynicism and sardonic
comment, you're prepared to swear you saw

first, a comet across your own stretch
of sky: second, a fallen angel trembling

like a raindrop on a leaf of green leather:
third, jumping out of her skin in the Verdi

Requiem, leaving her scales for someone
who might happen across a ploughed field

of sopranos, a lady in a cloudburst
of baritones who ended up dripping from a line:

basses and mezzos with criminal records
who have just decided to reform and set up

communes in rural areas: allowing for
the fact that they'll be terrified of the dark

pulverising of their hearts when they hear
sundry strolling operatic groups improvising

over an open fire. The lake-gatherers
queue, buy pencils and pots of jam,

scarcely able to take in that the find
of graphite at Borrowdale was at first

mistaken for coal. Heavy industry was ready
to roll in and take over until the samples

came back marked you must be joking.
Snaking for cover, for the curled-up ferns

and rock crevices, the clattering scree,
the still sea and shale beach: impressions

of shingle on your extremities
and someone in a cave's missing top C.

Someone beside the rock pool's attacked
by a crab and killer kelp as the tide

lifts in reinforcements. They put up
the red flag to tell you not to swim.

Con

Creeping through the crypt in size nines,
the resurrection men: carpenters,
plumbers, plasterers, masons, mummers
with no particular axe to grind.

Some pews needed to be ripped out,
some tombs necessarily disturbed:
this one, though, was renovation
at its loftiest. Everyone was about to be

uplifted. Cornelius had been buried here
some centuries before and his remains
were almost powder. When the lid
was off the skull retained its red hair

as if someone had draped a theatrical
wig over a hereditary peer. The workmen
made no bones, they were looking for
rings on fingers and bells on toes

and the claw hammer rested where once
there had been a nose. The head shifted,
came away in his hand. An idea
was born. He took a pole and raised

Cornelius up to face the man who
promptly had a heart attack. When asked
later if he regretted it, he said no,
I never liked him. And quiet returned.

Shakespeare In School

In her classroom she became Cassius
because her teacher wanted to suggest
she talked too much, conspiratorially,
and that this was best remedied by iron

discipline which involved long passages
of incomprehensible adult words
memorised mostly for no reason. Later
she became all the daughters of King Lear

as well as someone for whom Lady Macbeth
offered no surprise. Even in bobbie socks
professional footballers also wore, she shone
in her role until Miss became jealous, threw

a tantrum and one of those board duster
missiles to remind you to concentrate
on the matter in hand and not play truant
for any forthcoming month of Sundays.

In our classroom we were allocated
our parts as if in a toy factory,
with toy fights and skirmishes, lying low
one minute, protesting the next, hoping

for a line that would pass into legend,
that would light up the firmament or snare
small birds in flight. But all our recruitment
amounted to was to say Antony

and Cleopatra: not sure whether I
am Enobarbus or Dolabella, whether
the rumours about Servilia prostituting
her offspring to Caesar bore any truth.

During routine assassination scenes
you should try to establish clarity,
otherwise it's another free-for-all
with pieces of chalk flying everywhere.

Dividing Siamese Twins

The parents, given time to reflect,
showed a bewildering dignity,
gentle in their reservations, calm

in their acceptance of judicial
ruling, wayward in their emotion
like any sane person asked to do

something impossible, being told
that it is not only possible,
but there's a foreseeable

future beyond twenty past twelve.
Theatre lights, and journalists
imagining tomorrow's review.

An obsession with the time taken,
different times, like the disparity
between the number of lost planes

and ships and personnel. At war
with one another, the networks
concentrate on images of

a tiny hand, curling fingers.
The surgeons for once confessing,
taking off their masks and saying

of course they had doubts and also
of course it was a professional
challenge, but they were not dry ice

or godlike or any other
story likely to run and run.
The father will not be enticed

into recrimination: instead,
he looks forward to taking (in
his own words) one daughter home.

The mother's beautiful fractured
English gives her the chance to
say she feels her surviving

child senses something missing:
someone taken in the night
and separated forever.

Lisa Cannon

I grew up in Chepstow, South Wales and have always had a vivid imagination and a passion for writing. At school I had always loved poetry but never had the confidence to explore my interests. An inspirational English teacher encouraged me to write, not just poetry but also non fiction prose and short stories as well. Aged fifteen, I often found my poetry and prose did not follow expected teenage themes, and I submitted GCSE coursework entries concerning issues such as parricide, domestic abuse and human conditioning!

At university I was introduced to many new poets and writing opportunities and started to seriously collate the poems I produced. I continued to write when I left university and moved to London but found that working life meant I wasn't as prolific as in earlier years.

I find that I rarely write poetry when I am happy and many of my poems have served as a cathartic process throughout the years. I find that writing poetry allows me to say things I may not have the courage to say out loud and also clarifies my emotions.

I tend to write about personal events and issues that touch me, but occasionally I explore themes that friends or family are experiencing as a way of empathising and reaching out to them. I am finding that as the years roll by I am becoming less angry and more accepting of the world and I hope that this will lead to more optimistic poetry in the future.

There will never be a time when I don't write poetry; it's always within me and the process is usually effortless. It's part of who I am.

Falling

Green eyes.
Sea of insecurity
and doubt.
Shall I trust you?
Should I love you?
Too late;
I have drowned
and your eyes
are shut.

The Seven Year Itch

Who led me to this charmless life?
To the black witted demon who chained me here?
A sleeping beauty who did not see
how bland he had become to me.

How many years have I wallowed in this daze?
This married haze?

Once, he excited me,
his poison dripping like honey
all over my new red shoes.

You'll find my smile at the end of the rainbow
and my heart buried in the garden.
I won't be needing them anymore.

Sad faced and grey eyed,
I'm leaving,
with my old red shoes and half a regret.
Goodbye chains.
Goodbye honey.
Goodbye to the devil who makes me
itch, itch, *itch!*

The Mantrap

Shameless;
almost contorted.
He swears when he reaches the sky.
She swears when he leaves,
and he always leaves.

They call it love.
It's only justified if it's titled.
They'll learn.

Happiness;
teasingly reachable.
See the flowers smile
as clasped hands claw.
She'll always be scarred.

Her mother disapproves.
Her father doesn't know.
He will.

Bitterness;
sadly inevitable.
She says she'll never forgive him.
He tries to feel guilty
as he spies the next conquest.

See the pale, drawn woman
pop pill, and vodka, and pill.
See the trap.

My A-Z

Sometimes,
when lost,
I look to you.
I see a map
in your eyes
and a pathway
in your smile.

You are my key,
my direction,
my password.
You unlock me
and free me.

I love you.

She

Scarlet can be blinding,
But so can green.
See it crawl across the blinkers.
See it trail and creep
Its suspicious way
Through the heart.
See it kill trust
And diminish love.
Watch it,
And learn.

Nothing is immortal,
Or irreplacable,
But this hurt is irreversible.
It feeds paranoia,
Loves hate.
See the water well and fall,
The comforter discarded,
Because nothing soothes,
Nothing soothes,
Nothing.

The Entertainer

As if I should have known.
As if I was to blame;
Women always are.
See my heart bleeding?
See those tears falling?
One for you
One for your lies
One for your cruelty.
One day, they'll
Fall for someone else,
But today
They're just for you.
As if you'd even appreciate that.
As if you ever cared.

Unrequited

No leaves;
the trees are preparing for wintering.
For the cold, harsh winds,
the bitter, icy teardrops,
flowing in rivers of pearly white.

My heart
also feels the end of the end;
it's beating replacing the
fading pulse of the sun.
I wish you could love me.

Lunar

Every time I see red
I know I've failed again.
Looking down, miserably
tearfully, dejectedly.

Strands of hope
breaking free,
when together, they could form
the roots of my creation.

Pain wracks my stomach,
crouching down,
curling up tightly,
into myself.

Whiter pain fills my head.
Facing him again, explaining again.
It's all gone wrong, love,
It's all gone wrong.

Others manage it,
mannequins with no style,
no taste for the
choice they're given.

Such a waste.
I am void.
empty in all senses,
except in the need.

The need to fulfil,
the need to give,
my one wish.
That smiling reflection,
that tiny copy of me.

Time to start again.

Blinded

Blinded,
by complete darkness
and uncertainty.
Eternity chases behind,
safety lies ahead.
She beckons me,
and yet Death
sits at my shoulder.
Intriguing, persuading,
compelling.
He also knows my name.

The mirror
reflects my nothingness.
It has an opinion now;
but now it is too late,
I've made my choice.
I step back, into Death's shadow.
Desolation engulfs me
and Safety's smile fades.
She can't reach me,
and her trusting arms
seem as far away as home.

The Beach Dwellers

Darting eyes, probing glances,
nonchalantly obsessed.
Flesh
teasing their empty hearts,
their hollow fantasies.
Weary onlookers pity them
and their hunger;
their need to see the unobtainable.
They are never satisfied
with their beach dwelling,
their prying.
They trudge on.
Tired legs and hot heads,
but worth it.
So very worth it.

Rat Racers

We walk along
the same grey lines,
thinking we are different.
How naïve.

Blank faces filter
through the tube.
We feign abstract moves,
all similar.

Twisted buildings,
empty grey boxes.
Soon filled with our frustration,
yet again.

Filing into doom,
anxiety and stress.
Teatime an eternity away yet
thankfully inevitable.

Join this race
if you wish.
There are no winners, no prizes.
Just money.

Take heed.
Watch our tired faces,
see the weariness in our pinstripes,
see our high heels drag,
see the desperation,
see what we do . . .
and learn,
how valuable,
some paper can be.

Hope Less

It's hard to stop you when you've started,
And when you start you never stop.
Your anger rushing like a whirlwind,
A stream of rage, a vicious clot.
Your heart on fire, your eyes are black,
I know there is no turning back.

Your fists are flying, you deal your blows
I cower and shudder, your evil grows.
I see your fire, I see your soul,
It's like a huge and empty hole.
My vision blurred, my face now blue.
My epitome of fear is you.

My father hit my mother, so,
Perhaps this was the way to go.
To marry, to find someone who could
Beat me, like he knew he should.
I know my child will be the same,
We're masters at this endless game.

I see no freedom, I see no light,
I know the law, I have no right
To argue back, to dare defy,
The husband who will see me die.
He knows my terror, so beats again,
Absorbs my cries, ignores my shame.

I watch him leave and quietly pray,
That maybe, just maybe, today's the day,
That my dreams become reality
And I'll be taken from my misery.

Hours later you return, drunken and disgraced.
I slowly turn to meet your gaze, forgiveness on my face.

Nostalgia

Cut, chop, change.
Feel the child slip away.
Smile a wistful smile,
And move on.

You can always call her back.
Be mischievous.
Feel innocent and free.
She'll never die.

But be true to yourself.
You've changed.
No turning back,
You shouldn't want to.

Cut, chop, change.
Perfection is challenging,
So challenge.
Ghost child; new woman.

Shadows

Shadows of the past
remind me that
I am no longer innocent,
no longer free of guilt
and shame.
Destined to drive through
desolate streets solitary,
and despised.
Wanted, but not in
the needing sense.
Labelled as a misfit,
not worthy of God's life.
Fragmented beams of light
brighten my gloomy path,
suggesting a better life,
somewhere else
as someone else.
If only the shadows would
set me free.

Tors Taylor

I live in Siddington on the outskirts of the small town of Cirencester with my parents, but might be moving to outer London some time next year. I have lived in the same house all my life, and the walls are full of memories.

I first started writing poems when I was about 7 or 8, so have been writing poetry for around 9 years. I first had one of my poems published when I was 9 years old, with a Poetry Now book called 'Cosmic'. Different pieces of my work have also been published in 4 other compilations by Anchor Books and Young Writers.

I tend to write about any feelings I have been keeping inside, and things that have happened to me, my friends or my family, but sometimes the words just come to me and I end up writing a completely different sort of poem. I write a lot of poems about my gran and people that have affected my life in some way.

I like to write poetry because I write a lot of songs as I am a musician, and sometimes I'll write a song that would sound better as a poem and vice versa. I didn't write any poems for a couple of years but when my gran passed away, I found a collection of poems I had written for her and started writing again.

The Fight Against Life

Just because someone's fighting for their life
Doesn't mean there's anything wrong
It just means there's nothing right.

Sometimes all a person needs is a hug
And to know that they don't have to scream inside
- They're not gonna be heard anyway.

I once wrote on my wall, 'It's time for the good things
- No more of the bad'
And I've tried, I really have, but maybe for once I should just give in.
(Whoever wins anyway?)

I find life a really difficult thing,
You have to beat life before you can be alive.
I wanna reach up and strangle life, but I'm too far down on the ground,
In the dirt, with the worms,
But I can't reach high enough to kill life and stop it ruining me.

(If all of you are the damaged ones, then who am I?
I can't be one of you - I'm never accepted as anything.)

As long as I have life, I cannot be me, but without life I cannot be
(At all.)

(If I was to give in, would I even be a memory?)

Unknown Passion

No matter how hard I try, I can't seem to get to touch you,
To hold you close and smile at you and mean it.
This pain is killing me,
How come having so much lust for someone makes you so depressed?

Life's not fair and neither is the game of love.

I sit and wait and wonder
What it is that makes me love you
I don't even know you but
Certainty and love like this comes but once in a lifetime.
I need you.

There is nothing I can write
That hasn't been put in a song before,
Nothing I can say
That some stranger hasn't said before.
But I need you to know and I know this seems strange
Considering I've never let it show.

But you make me brain dead,
I can't help but stutter when I'm trying to talk to you.
I love you don't disappear.

On these lonely summer nights
I wish to hear your voice
I think about you, these thoughts never leave me
And they make me burst with passion.

Gimme everything you've got tonight
And then forever and a day
We may be young but honey that only gives us more time.
You're my medicine - give me you.

I want you now.

How do I tell you?
How will you react?
Don't brush me aside and think nothing of me
I know this is a cliché but no one will ever love you like I do.

I'm screaming inside needing to talk to you, to see you
Needing to tell someone about my love for you
Knowing I can't tell you cos you're nowhere near me
While you don't even notice me.

Not A Chance To Say . . . Goodbye

(You were my blood, and half of it has been taken, now there's only half of me and I'm too weak to survive.)

So now you're comfortable and safe
Tucked up in a cloud
You won't feel my anger, or feel my pain
The memories have drowned.

People say what we had was unique
And what we had was special
But you've passed away and so has a year
That day you made a mess of

I have found it hard to cope
Without you as a guide
There was an empty flat and my empty heart
That made it hard to smile.

My life, heart, my body and soul
Has broken like glass and still hasn't mended
I've tried to cope but broken down
To you I have offended.

I hope today you would be proud
And smile that cheery smile
I'd trade my life just to see you once more
I know it'd be worthwhile.

I miss the way you laugh
I miss the games we played
No longer can I cry to you
I only cry to heal my pain.

You left me and I wasn't ready
For you to leave my side
All I want is a hug from you
And the chance to say goodbye.

I slowly shattered into a thousand pieces
And was bitter and sharp like shards of glass
My heart is weak and it can't afford
To ever break again, cos it's
Just
Not
Strong
Enough
To
Mend.

Loving You

Loving you makes me feel alive
In my stomach I get butterflies
To fly away with you would be all right
Oh, if only you were mine.

Your voice is like an angel's whisper
It makes my heart hurt like a blister
Once asleep I dream of you
Oh, if only you knew.

You make my head twist into a spin
I wish someone could help me with the mess that I'm in
That 'mess' being my love for you
But, there's simply nothing anyone else could ever do.

Gran

Sitting by your window
Early in the morn
Staring at the quiet world
Watching people come out at dawn.

Your books and papers bring comfort to you
Your mind is lost in thought
The days disappear 'til they're almost through -
A silent night is brought.

Falling asleep at night
Thoughts of the day fill your head
Listening to the sounds of the traffic
Until sleep makes the night dead.

Hating You

I hate every second spent with you
Time moves slowly - on and on
Commit myself to anger to hate you
My suicide day has come.

Give me peace, let me rest
I was once strong but I failed the test
The test of life, life filled with anger, hate, depression
My suicidal tendencies become more frequent.

I choose my life - my life is me
Exactly how I want to be
No one will change that, it's not a phase
And as I'm happy, your thoughts of me should be erased.

So you have a problem with who I am
Have you ever stopped to think about who you are?
Not everyone wants to look like you - sparkly and glam
So your attitude to me could be lighter by far.

Gone With The Wind

Gone forever, never coming back
Like a bird in the wind her wings have flapped
In the house of the lords is where she did pray
'Til that fatal night when it was where she lay.

To think of happy times that we did have
And to know that they are never coming back
Brings great sadness to my world
The thoughts in my mind twirl and swirl.

I need release from the arms of this living hell
I need to feel happy and know that all's well
But living without her hurts me so bad
Half of me is missing and will never come back.

We were very close and her death's made me sad
I am not myself, my world's rotten - gone bad
But still I live on in this misery
And face each day being unhappy.

To say this is hard is an understatement
I need some reassurance but nothing helps
I can never move on just live on with my mind bent
Forever she is gone not worrying how I've felt.

I wrote her poems, I read her stories
I helped her out with jobs at home
We had so many pacts and special places
But nearly all of that is gone.

On Christmas day - I will never forget
This tragedy - like cement - did set
And so her life is no more to be
I'll always love you Gran - RIP.

Suffering

There's a little girl, she lives down my lane
I think that she's dying, dying in pain.
And that little girl feels so alone,
She cries every night when her parents aren't home.

She wishes her life away
Sometimes she wishes she was dead,
And that brings the pain and the spinning in her head.
She's got so depressed, that it's killing her slowly,
There's blood on her dress,
She needs a new one - if only!

Her parents don't care, wishes she weren't there.
So they make her life hell,
And at school she doesn't do well.
She's got no social life, not even at school,
She's bullied and hated; no kids think she's cool.

So inside she's rotting, rotting away,
And she's dying now, because of the pain.

Xmas

It is a time for joy and happiness,
I used to really love this thing called Xmas.
But since last year I'm not so sure,
That it's really that great anymore.

I used to dream about Xmas Eve,
You see, I could never wait
But now Xmas is my time to grieve
And I don't look forward to that date.

It was 25th of December 2002
I woke at 6am - very excited, and the day started off great!
Then my mum got the phone call, she didn't know what to do,
I went and woke Dad up - not knowing our fate.

So it's 4 months later now
I'm getting through it - how?
Things will never be the same
And I'm dreading Xmas, but in 8 months it'll be that time of year again.

Dying World

Living a life in hope, in pain,
Wanting out, saying never again.

Everyone's fake, making their life something unreal,
But once they're all alone the truth is unsealed.
Stop the anger, hate the pain, just give up I can't contain.

I have shed the tears
And I have bled the fears,
Of this dying world.

I won't be a bore,
I can't take no more.
I'm going down the drain,
I don't want no more,
I'm just a bore.
I'm twisted, confused - insane.

I had the lonely child's heart
There was nothing left to give
I had sat and waited - listened
But all I could do was grieve.

Over my life
Over my world
Over the time
All of which was dead and gone.

I'd lived this way,
I'd lived that way,
And now I'm giving up.

Dreams

My dreams are unreal,
Yet seem more real than my life,
Being awake is like a nightmare,
Everything is perfect in a dream.

Sometimes it's sad when I wake up,
My dreams are always interrupted by the voice that hates me.
It's my conscience trying to tell me something -
And my spirit trying to break free.

What am I? Just a dream.

Inspiration

Through thick and thin it was there
Helping me to grow to be what I am.
Seeking the help when I couldn't bare
To face the outer world.
Like an SOS the music was there
Making me strong so I didn't turn to air.

It followed me when I was angry
It smiled at me when I was sad
It was there when I was happy
For the music I am glad.

When the rain falls down on misery
It only makes me weep
When the sun is shining my heart fills up
Inspiration is forever to keep.

The mind works in an unsolved manner
Mysterious and spiralling downhill,
Not thinking about our past regrets
Will only fool us into cheap thrills.

Joseph Tafadzwa Musamadya Nthini

My name is Joseph Musamadya Nthini and I'm a young African man aged 28 years. As a child I loved to read books and consequently I took up writing and got hooked to words. It provided an escape from reality and boredom. I enjoyed seeing my stories being published in school magazines and read out to different classes.

I realised my potential and talent through the patient guidance and mentoring of my late English teacher, Mr Mugandani. He encouraged me to carry on writing and so I have done so.

I've worked as a scriptwriter and researcher for TV production companies which I enjoyed but deep down I wanted to create something of my own. I guess my writer's voice was calling.

I struggled to find things to write about but then tragedy struck and I lost my young sister. It hit me hard and I fell rock bottom. From my loss I gained strength to articulate myself and my feelings and heal myself through the power of words. Also during the same period I went through a lot of very harsh challenges and trials, and a few triumphs but mostly it was hell. This inspired me to search deeper within my soul and heart. This articulate conception is partly a result of that phase. It contains fragments of my mind, moments captured by the lens of my soul and immortalised in this body of work. It contains Thank You Mama printed in Expressions from London and Home Counties 2004 by Anchor Books.

I am also currently working on my debut novel The Rising Sun, circumstances permitting it should be completed next year. By getting my poetry published I hope to leave a legacy of words for my family and descendants. I hope to leave a lasting legacy of my thoughts, words and works for my family, friends, descendants and world at large.

Thank You Mama

Thank you Mama for all you've been through
But you still remain pure and true;
Mama you've really done your best
It's not your fault if I turn out the worst,
Have no fear cos at times things may be hard
Yet I know that one day you'll get your reward.
I know the Lord sees your tears and hears your prayers
And he's been there for you throughout all these years;
You raised us the best way you could
Although we didn't live in the greatest neighbourhood.
Even when there was no money you kept us in school
Because you didn't want us to grow up to be fools.
Sometimes Daddy was never around
But as a single mum you raised us up real good
Even when the pantry had little food.
I wish everyone had a mother with so much love
Peaceful, beautiful and sweeter than a dove;
Even when things are tough and really bad
You help me absorb the pressures of life together with Dad.
I just want you to know that I really appreciate -
My love and respect for you will never ever depreciate.
Whenever I'm down and can't face the raging storm
You're always by my side encouraging and keeping me warm;
Mum I love you and I want to say thanks for everything
That's why I write this verse to let you know how I'm feeling.

Reggae Music I

I see the B-man fighting to dominate the world
And He rallies law and government institutions
To fight and beat black people down.

B-man doesn't want us to listen to reggae music
And wants to ban it from radio and record stores
But Jah knows, He's raging in vain.

Reggae music burns out B-man's corrupt ways
Cos the music lightens up their wicked works
So dem nah waan see reggae music a gwaan.

B-man issuing out warrants of arrest to mute Jah prophets
But minus Reggae music they're still living in sin,
And can't stop Reggae music and we fi sing 'bout dis ting.

Do you hear me B-man?
You can't stop we fi sing
Praises to the Most High King.

You can't stop we singing about the racial divide
Oh no! You can't stop the course of time and tide.
Oh sinner man where will you run and hide?

Turn up the base and treble on the hi-fi
Cos this is fire burning Iyah.
It's so sweet and I feel irie.

Tunn it up and burn the fire
Cos B-man a go tire
Cos we're stepping up higher.

B-man it's time to change your wicked ways -
Get on your knees and give Jah thanks and praise
Cah me tell boogaman, fire nuh done blaze.

Reggae Music II

Mercenaries destroyed our homes, stole our gold
Reggae music we own it cos we create it
And white man never mek it but waan brek it.
I don't care what Twitter Satchell says
Sweet reggae music, the natural mystic must play.

I waan listen to da word, sound and power in da base
And give Jah thanks and praise cah fire haffi blaze -
That's why the heathen and outrage continue to rage
But they're living and fighting in vain.
Dem are go tired fi see we face
But can't get Natty Dread outta de race.

On their plantations they whipped us to pick cotton
Till we dropped down dead and our hands rotten;
If we ever did try to escape and run
It was out with the dog and the gun
But all we've got left is Reggae and it can't stop.

Mad sick, nah no head, Reggae in my head
I take it like my daily bread,
They're fighting for gay rights, wonder which God demma praise?
Reggae music is all we got left and it haffi blaze
Cos Reggae music can't stop and there's no time to gaze
Come Natty and fight for your rights against bumboclaat gays.

Reggae music never ever promote no violence
If you don't understand the message, shut up and give me silence
Reggae is conscious music with a positive black message
Cos Natty Dread is a priest spreading Rasta knowledge.
Tell Twitter Satchell and outrage to stop fight Natty Dread
Cos Reggae music must continue to scatter and spread.

Mother

M ama you're my shining star and
O nly your love is true despite all my faults.
T he worldly ills are a bed of roses with you;
H ear what I say Mama cos I appreciate
E ven when times were hard you made ends meet
R espect is due for the miracles you worked Mama.

M ama thanks for all you've done
O nly God knows the hell you went through,
T hanks for the nine months you carried me as
H aving me is the best thing you did for me.
E ven though your life hasn't been easy, I
R emember the hard times when you fought to keep us as one.

M ama you've done your best but now it's
O ur time to do the rest cos I recall
T imes when Daddy was never around, but,
H ow you managed to play both roles baffles me,
E ven though the world may frown down at you -
R everence and respect is all I've got for you.

M ama don't worry, better days will soon come so
O pen your eyes and wipe away your tears,
T he Good Lord hears your liquid prayers.
H e will guide and protect us as He's always done.
E very mother is her son's greatest heroine, so Mum
R espect and Love to you the Queen of my heart.

Power Vice

How can we go on like this?
It's time that we've some peace
For this grip onto power must ease
And the violence and intimidation cease.

Sometimes I wonder how leaders sleep at night
Knowing that poor people have no food to eat
But they spend millions without sweating for it
Yet children are sleeping out on the streets.

Leaders fly high with their egos on multi-million dollar shopping sprees
Yet the violence and intimidation they can't appease.
Poor people can't afford brainwashed education and exorbitant fees
And youths dropout daily but one day they'll have you on your knees.

I see the hidden writing there upon the wall
And your pride proceeds your nasty fall,
When the tables turn who are you going to call?
When you're down and being kicked like a damn football.

The country's economy is in its worst ever recession
Yet you amend and bend the fragile constitution
Causing poor people and the youths so much frustration
But one day you shall pay for your intimidation and corruption.

The signs of a revolution are right in front of your eyes
Yet you conveniently choose to ignore the sufferer's cries
And try to blind your hideous crimes with your scandalous lies
But beware because people are getting wise and you'll pay
for your crimes.

Your Love

Loving you is so scandalous
Cos they say that you're a seductress;
So for me to be with you
I must stand up for what I choose.
All I seek is my heart's joy
But they say that what you touch you destroy.
If we could go back in time
Maybe we could change our past and life;
If being with you is wrong
Then I'd rather be alone.

Your Love makes me so happy
But our liaison makes our families unhappy;
Love is truly something to treasure
And I wonder what scale they use to measure.
If only they knew how you make me feel -
Our love's real, maybe they'd let us follow our will.
Just because you're slightly older
Doesn't mean you can't be my lover,
By chance should they see us together
They wouldn't even have to bother.

Your love means I have to cut family ties
To avoid living a life of conflict and lies,
Your love has come at a terrible cost
Cos I'm now branded as one who's lost,
You love brings me so much agony
And puts me through conflict and antagony.
Your love has made my life a mess
But if I must confess of all the times, this is the best.

Highest Grade

Give me the highest grade
And let me blaze
I got to burn it everyday
Don't care what people say.

A friend in weed
Is a friend indeed
Smoke till we eyes them bleed,
But don't burn up the seed
Cos we don't kill the breed.

I take it like tea
And if you ask me how I feel?
I'm fine and feeling free
Just like I wanna be.

Gimme the highest grade
I'll smoke it when I crave
It was found on King Solomon's grave
So I'll give thanks and praise
To the ancient of days.

I'm burning the highest grade
And it's in my head.

Until

Until black on black crime is eradicated and totally annihilated,
stop nipping the Black Rose in the bud before it blooms;
Until you give us the teachings of His Majesty and utterly obliterate
the Devil's philosophy;
Until we all stand in the eyes of God and man as equals
not as first and second class citizens of any nation,
Until the preachers start to preach peace, truth and love without a lie
in their hearts to provide salvation for those that seek God;
Until the children can run and play in the park freely without fear
of gunshots barking in the park,
Until we learn to share and start giving instead of just receiving
and taking the corn where we did not sow,
Until we're judged by the quality of our intelligence and not
by the colour of skin or the texture of our hair,
Until we're free by any means necessary and independent politically,
economically and spiritually,
Until these dis-united nations unite and start to uplift the nation
pushing for true I-nification (unification),
Until Africa comes together and we unite and create the United States
of Africa as the spiritual utopia of Africans at home and abroad,
Until One Love is finally and permanently realised and accomplished,
we don't need no democracy or man made laws to control
and rule people,
Until we achieve what we will we mighty race of people and Nubian
Kings and Queens finally reclaim their righteous throne in the world;
Until they give us more opportunity in the shit-stem (system) and
society where we don't have to protest and steal to make ends meet,
Until they stop fighting the terrible terror war and destroy their
biological and nuclear gear cos we don't want any nuclear war.
Until their Bobbies stop stopping us on the streets soliciting
for a search and trapping us at their road blocks,
Until they cease beating us with their truncheons and shooting us
with their brutal glocks cos when they shoot and kill a nigger
they think they're heroes,

Until they find a remedy for neo-colonisation and corruption festering
like a cancerous chancre,
Until we liberate our minds from mental slavery and they release
the chains from our brains and free us from the lion's den;
Until they stop the senseless violence and killing without a cause
and start healing -
Until the day we don't have to fight for our rights cos they're using
might to try and beat right and block out the light,
Until we all unite and live in harmony,
Until then, this world will know no peace.

Little Rose

Hazel dreamy eyes, olive skin, golden blonde tresses
'Mini skirts, track suits, jeans, thongs, not floral dresses
Are the thing for me,' say Little Rose,
But animosity and conflict deny her the right to choose.
Paedophiles, zit faced teens, oily hair and lust crazed men
Court, drag and propose to her as if she's a woman.
God! Don't they see that she is only a child at thirteen?
But she already knows the odour and taste of semen.

Semen spoiled pants, soiled bra, blood-stained frock;
Rose is numb, oblivious and used to abuse on the block.
Who really does give a f**k?
If Dick, Tom and Harry she must suck
Just to get a roof over her head
And maybe, a slice of her daily bread.
She's done it with every curious lad
So everyone labels her a slag, a guaranteed shag.

Out on the street Little Rose must roam
Cos it's world war four and hell at home,
Rose is searching for somewhere to belong
But people shun her not knowing where she's from,
A silent, unwilling victim of child abuse
She ain't got the privilege to deny or choose
Rose needs someone to lovingly guide and nudge her
Not anyone to unknowingly and blind, come to judge her.

Little Rose is from a broken home and it isn't easy on her own
When we torture her soul and push her further down the hole.
She's seeking an answer to why she's so sad, black and blue
But nightmares, abuse and heaving bodies oppress her, she ain't got a clue.
Sometimes I wonder what's Rose's future,
When she needs someone not to abuse her but teach her.

Irrelevant Rhyme

Irrelevant rhyme is a poet's greatest crime
They write for form not for the love or fun,
If it doesn't make sense
Must be poets in pretence,
If it carries no feeling
I know it has no meaning.
Some write from the head
But I write from my heart,
Check how me rhyming
Same time you get my meaning -
So if it doesn't make sense
It must be nonsense.

I don't know much about style or punctuation
Cos I write to vent my pent up emotion,
So clean up the act
And bring good old simple writing back -
Because irrelevant rhyme is a crime
A waste of lines and time.
Breath life and feeling into the scribes
And create some good vibes and good lines.
If it has feeling
Then it has meaning -
Write to show off
And write yourself off.

'Tis so outta season
Obscuring all reason.

Spotlight Poets Information

We hope you have enjoyed reading this book - and that you will continue to enjoy it in the coming years.

If you are interested in becoming a Spotlight Poet then drop us a line, or give us a call, and we'll send you a free information pack.

Alternatively if you would like to order further copies of this book or any of our other titles, then please give us a call or visit our website at www.forwardpress.co.uk

Spotlight
Poets

Spotlight Poets Information
Remus House
Coltsfoot Drive
Peterborough
PE2 9JX

Telephone: 01733 898102

Email: spotlightpoets@forwardpress.co.uk